SUBMIT
IS NOT A
FOUR-LETTER
WORD

Submit to Get the Relationship You
Want with God (and Your Husband)

Laura Provencio

WESTBOW
PRESS®
A DIVISION OF THOMAS NELSON
& ZONDERVAN

WestBow Press books may be ordered through booksellers or by contacting:

WestBow Press
A Division of Thomas Nelson & Zondervan
1663 Liberty Drive
Bloomington, IN 47403
www.westbowpress.com
1 (866) 928-1240

ISBN: 978-1-9736-8315-5 (sc)
ISBN: 978-1-9736-8314-8 (e)

Library of Congress Control Number: 2020900310

Print information available on the last page.

WestBow Press rev. date: 01/22/2020

This book is dedicated to my loving husband, Paul.
His artistic soul inspires my practical one.

Contents

Preface

This book started out as a diary entry. I was reading the book *Sacred Marriage* by Gary Thomas and felt convicted to put real submission into practice. I started by examining how I behaved as a wife and writing down what I was learning. Each time I submitted to my husband, God blessed me. It seemed unreal. I had to document my growth, especially after sixteen years of marriage!

These life lessons about submission slowly turned into chapters, which then turned into a whole book. I enjoy encouraging others, and I hope this book helps wives to submit to God and their husbands. It's been extremely beneficial to my walk with the Lord. It has been an even bigger blessing to my marriage. God knows exactly what He is doing. Trust in Him.

Introduction

> I will greatly rejoice in the Lord, my soul shall be
> joyful in my God.
>
> —Isaiah 61:10

Submit may seem like a four-letter-word to you, but it is the answer. Have you ever wondered why you do not feel the joy of the Lord in your life? We sing it in church, we read it in our Bibles, but we just don't feel it. Submitting to God is the answer.

When I actually stopped and thought about why I do the things I do, it was very eye opening. First, I realized that most of the things I do, God did not ask me to do, my husband did not ask me to do, and even my kids did not ask me to do. I had set up this expectation of myself that I could not reach. I just kept trying to reach it. It was an ideal of perfection. I was striving toward it, not toward God.

The biblical truth of submission is always preached cautiously at church. Everyone seems to cringe when the word is mentioned. We all seem to think, *Yeah, right.* But when you look more closely at the Scriptures, submission is actually for our benefit. Yes, it's true. The idea of letting someone tell me what to do seems just wrong. I do not like being told what to do. At all. Yet at the same time, I'm good at following directions. But submit, that just sounds bad.

The truths shared in this book will encourage you to submit. Let me tell you ahead of time, "Surrender now." It will save you a lot of heartache. Even if it goes against every grain in your body, do it. Listen to the Lord and His Word. Submit to Him to get the abundant life He has promised.

Chapter 1
Trust in the Lord

I was missing the joy in my walk with God. I didn't know where it went. I knew it was in the Bible somewhere, and I read my Bible daily to find it. Yet I wasn't feeling any of it. God met me right where I was to show me that the way to joy is through submission. To open my eyes to trust Him and surrender, God used the people directly around me—my family. God used my kids first because I love my kids unconditionally. And God knows me.

It was summertime, and I was shaken to my core with the fact that both of my kids were going to be in junior high. I didn't expect to be confronted with all the emotions that filled me. I trained my kids to be independent and to trust in the Lord. Now they were walking in that independence. This made me realize that I had basically done my job as a mother. I raised them, and now they were walking forward. This terrified me. I felt like I had lost control of their lives. I know that technically I did not ever have control of their lives, but I guess I thought I did.

Little did I know that God was going to turn me upside down. I felt lost now that my kids were in junior high. What was my job now? What should I do? How does this all work? Well, God brought me to my knees. He knew that I did not trust my kids in His wonderful hands. I did not trust that God could take care of them better than I could. That's the honest truth. When God reminded me of my favorite verse in the Bible, I had a hard time embracing the truth of it in regard to my kids.

> Trust in the Lord with all your heart and lean not on your own understanding. In all your ways acknowledge Him, and He will direct your paths. (Proverbs 3:5–6)

I have written this verse everywhere. I memorized this verse at a young age, and I thought I knew it through and through. Boy was I wrong. Trusting the Lord with my kids is a tough one. Especially when you are trying so hard to be the perfect mother and wife, even though God never asked you to. The truth of this Bible verse helped me to let go of my kids and open my hands to God. It's a daily choice. It's not easy, but seeing the fruit of the Lord in my children's lives is priceless. They are thriving, and I have stepped back. They are truly in God's hands, and He is working in their lives. He is God; I am not. Who do I think I am?

I am the Lord's. Only through trusting Him and submitting to His will for my life will I be able to embrace the joy He has for me. My children are a gift to me. They are also a tool God uses to refine me in my walk with Him. Trust and submission go hand in hand. The more I trust in the Lord, the more I can be an effective mother to my children as they are growing up.

Chapter 2
Practical Submission

Submitting to your husband is preached from the pulpit maybe twice a year—and very carefully. As God was refining me to trust in and submit to Him, He used my husband to teach me. God did it gently and clearly.

We were driving home from a fun family day at Venice Beach when my sweet husband mentioned that I was not good at following him when we danced the two-step. He shared these words with me after my daughter accused me of not following Dad while we were walking on the boardwalk. I took his words to a whole new level. How dare he say I am not good at following him! I follow him every day, or so I thought.

I decided right there and then that I would prove to myself that I followed my husband. The very next morning I said no to him twice. I walked away from him when he was talking to me, and this shocked me. I really thought I was following him like a good wife should. I thought I was a submissive woman. Not even close. I made a choice to start submitting to my husband in practical ways, in real ways. Like for real.

I submitted paying the bills to my husband as my first big

step. I took a deep breath and asked him if he would take over the chore of paying the bills. He agreed, and I felt like a huge burden was lifted off my shoulders. Not only did he start taking care of the bills, he was better at it than I was! He even saved enough money for our family to go to Hawaii. I was only able to save enough money for Little Caesars pizza every Friday night.

I knew that it would be easy for me to submit to God because He is God. I knew that I could trust in the Lord. I didn't know if I could submit to my husband full time. I wanted to do it. I wanted to prove that it was possible. So I started by listening to him. Yes, listening to my husband.

We woke up one morning, and as he got up, he said, "Stay in bed and sleep." Normally I would've gotten up along with him and ignored his direction. But this time I listened. I stayed in bed and slept. It was wonderful. It was so nice. I never allowed myself this luxury, and my handsome husband suggested it. Wow! I never thought that listening to my husband would be a blessing to me. I always thought of submitting as a chore, a job, something I didn't want to do. Now here I was, sleeping in. All because I listened to my husband and submitted to his direction. I did not anticipate this at all.

I started submitting more to my husband, listening to his directions and following them. In turn, my husband started changing. He started hugging me more (which I love) and making me breakfast. He put his hand on my back as we walked together. He was being tender with me as I was submitting to him. It was overwhelming and strange. I didn't think my little changes would change my husband as well.

I guess what I'm learning is that God's ways are a blessing, not burdensome. When I do what the Bible says to do, there is real fruit. As I put God's Word into practice with regards to my husband, my husband was putting into practice God's Word regarding me. Once again, God is faithful. His ways are not our ways; they are better!

Chapter 3
Change, the Other Four-Letter Word

As God was teaching me to embrace change and trust Him with my kids, He was also teaching me to submit to Him. Trust and submission go hand in hand. I was trusting God with my kids and now trusting God with my marriage, doing marriage God's way. Just like the following verse says:

> Wives, submit to your own husbands, as to the Lord. (Ephesians 5:22)

Submitting to the Lord is the first step. Trusting your life to the Lord's hands is what you need to do. Believe in Jesus. He will give you eternal life.

> For God so loved the world that He gave His only begotten Son, that whoever believes in Him, will not perish, but have eternal life. (John 3:16)

That is what God asks of you. Believe in Him. He sent Jesus as a gift for us. Through Jesus we have eternal life. He is the only way. Trust in Him, and He will direct your path. This is the first step to joy, joy in the Lord.

Now, as you submit to the Lord, you are in the right mindset to submit to your husband, submit to those in authority, and so on. Getting your priorities in line with God's will for your life starts with Jesus.

Putting these things into practice is the next step. We can say anything we want; walking in those ways is the true test. It's practical application. It's peace. It's truly how God wants us to relate to Him. There is contentment as we submit to God and trust in Him, not in our ways. He is faithful to help you every step of the way. He will not let you down. He wants you to walk in His ways. He wants you to go forward. He gives you the tools through His Word and expects you to walk in them. That's the hard part.

The blessings that take place as you walk in God's ways feel like a reward. You have to walk by faith and not by sight. You have to put it into practice. This means change. Yes, the other four-letter word.

Change is a constant in our lives. We can actually count on change. Change will happen whether we want it to or not. Embracing change is ideal. Fighting change is not. Most of our emotional and mental struggles are with change. Either we look back on our lives to the should haves, which leads to depression, or we wonder about our tomorrows and the what-ifs, which leads to anxiety. Both of these are not helpful. We need to live each day in the present. Today.

Chapter 4
The Dance

I started out wanting to be submissive to my husband because he told me I was not good at following him when we danced the two-step. I really thought I was good at following him. Well, we had a chance to try out the two-step at a New Year's Eve dance. My mother-in-law and father-in-law are both in a band that plays on New Year's Eve in their barn in Arizona. Since I'd been putting full-time submission into practice with my husband for a few weeks by then—with very positive results—I was ready for the dance.

The funny thing is while I was getting ready for the dance, I felt such peace. I remember going to this dance the year prior and really wanting to dance with my husband. I kept asking him, "When are we going to dance?" I was basically nagging him to dance. I wanted to dance so bad, and I didn't understand why my husband wasn't leading me on to the dance floor. I think we only danced once or twice that night, and I felt disappointed. I had envisioned dancing the whole night.

Well, this new feeling of peace from practicing submission and waiting on the Lord felt relaxing. No stress, no anxiety, and no expectation for the night, just peace. It felt so good. I got ready for the dance and walked into the barn. (Yes, it was a barn dance with my in-law's country band.) My husband greeted me and gave me a kiss. The band started playing their first song, and my husband led me to the dance floor to dance. He took my hand and led me. Let me write that again. He took my hand and led me. I didn't have to wish hard for him to understand that I needed to dance. I didn't have to nag him or suggest ideas for him. He led me. This is how God blesses when we submit.

God blessed my night with my husband. I was filled with peace, not anticipation of some expectation. My husband led me to the dance floor, and I followed. We danced together with all the tenderness I remember from when we were dating. My handsome husband led me around the dance floor, and I followed his lead. We were able to dance the two-step because I was following my husband's lead. I was relaxed and enjoying the beautiful dance. My husband even whispered into my ear that he loved me. This is what real submission looks like. A beautiful dance where two people are waltzing together in harmony. It looks smooth, and it feels wonderful. Just how God created marriage to be.

Chapter 5
Open Your Hands and Let Go

Surrender. Submit. The terms are interchangeable. It's all about surrendering yourself to God. To His will for your life. Not your way, but God's way. It's putting His Word into practice. Doing what the Bible says. Deuteronomy 8 is the perfect illustration of surrender. God's wisdom for us is to submit ourselves to Him.

> So you shall keep the commandments of the Lord
> your God by walking in his ways and by fearing
> him. (Deuteronomy 8:6)

We wander in the desert land of our thoughts and our actions. God lets us wander. He is right there with you as you make choices without seeking Him. He still loves you. He wants you to submit to His will for your life, to surrender this idea of control at any level and trust in Him. Trust that He knows best in every situation. Even when it's hard and the tears are falling down, He is there. He wants us to get up and follow Him.

Only when we open our hands and let go of the things we are holding tightly to can we hold God's hands. His hands are always open to us. When we let go, we are able to hold on to God and His ways. The things we need to hold on to. His grace. His mercy. Not the things that weigh us down.

God gave us everything we need in the Bible. It is the way to walk with Him. It is the map for our Christian faith. It's not always easy, but it's always fruitful. When we walk in God's ways, He is pruning us for more fruit. He wants us to be humble all the time, not to quickly rely on ourselves the minute life doesn't seem so hard. When all is well, we forget God. God doesn't want that in our relationships with Him.

He wants to walk hand in hand with us through life. Together. God leading the way, and us submitting to His plans, which are for our good. Our good doesn't always look the way we thought it would. It just looks different. And that is okay. Change requires adjustment. Soak in the fact that change is constant and necessary. Time to let go of the unnecessary and seek God's ways. God is faithful to meet you right where you are. Submit to Him.

Chapter 6
Vulnerability

> There is no fear in love, but perfect love casts out
> fear. For fear has to do with punishment, and
> whoever fears has not been perfected in love. We
> love because He first loved us.
>
> —1 John 4:18–19

Vulnerability. The big part of getting over yourself and being submissive is this uncomfortable word *vulnerable*. The reason we don't like that word is because we are afraid of it. God's Word tells us that perfect love casts out fear. God's love toward us is perfect. We should not be afraid of God, who loves us perfectly. We confuse God's unconditional love toward us with how we think we need to love our spouses. Part of the dynamic of marriage is that we need God's divine nature in us, His Holy Spirit, in order to submit to our husbands. Because we know God's love for us is perfect, when we rely on His love to guide us into submission to Him, we can then, in turn, submit to our husbands more easily.

Back to the vulnerable part. In order to be submissive, we are going to have to be vulnerable. We are going to have to be real with our spouses. We have to show our true colors, which we have possibly been hiding all this time. To do that, we must face our fears of being vulnerable and share with our husbands. We must use real words to describe what we are feeling or even the truth about the reality that is before you. It is amazing to me that I could spend many years of my marriage thinking I was being vulnerable when, in reality, I was not. Being vulnerable means being raw before your spouse. Just like the beauty of sex within marriage, God wants us to be vulnerable with our words too.

Putting vulnerability into practice looks different for the wife and the husband. As a wife, being vulnerable to your husband means talking about the "hard stuff." Being honest in love. For a husband, being vulnerable means sharing your feelings. Both are not easy to do but extremely helpful in marriage. Communicating to each other in a friendly setting is how real issues get resolved.

Chapter 7
A New Kind of Normal

I think it's time to share how to handle the change within you as you submit to your husband. And things will really change. Things will look different in your marriage. This shift to your husband leading your family might make you feel like you've lost your job. This feeling is constantly in front of me. I thought it was my job to do everything.

Now that I am submitting to my husband, he is taking care of everything. He fills up the gas in my car, he tells the kids to brush their teeth, and he even initiates praying with them before bed. My independent nature doesn't know what to do with all this new free time. Not that it's a lot of free time. It's just that now my role as a wife is different. It's calmer. It's peaceful. It's not full of demands that I used to think were my responsibility. Now it's balanced in our home.

My husband leads our family, and I respect him. My job is to take care of the kids when he isn't home and defer to him when he is home. It's like relearning how to be a wife. Not that everything has changed, but my mentality has changed. I am not in control. Maybe my controlling nature was always behaving in a certain way, and now I have to retrain my brain to submit. It's a daily challenge. It's part of the whole process.

Thank heavens we have the Holy Spirit living in us to help us through it all. Staying stagnate in our old ways will only stifle our growth. Don't cling to the old ways; strive toward the new, and be patient with yourself. God finally did a work in you that is for your good, and now you can walk in it. You can enjoy being a wife and letting your husband pamper you like he did when you were dating. Don't fight the new feelings. Enjoy the blessings.

Chapter 8
R-E-S-P-E-C-T

> However, let each one of you love his wife as himself, and let the wife see that she respects her husband.
>
> —Ephesians 5:33

I just finished reading the book *Love & Respect* by Dr. Emerson Eggerichs. I had read about 75 percent of it a few years back and stopped because I disagreed with the author. Needless to say, when I opened it back up, I was ready to swallow what I read and choke on the conviction of it. God knew I would be ready to listen this time.

I have been focusing on submitting to my husband, but the main topic of the book was about respecting your husband. The verse from Ephesians 5:33 simply explains that husbands are to love their wives, and wives are to respect their husbands. It seems so simple, yet it's not that easy to do.

My husband and I went to our church's marriage couples' night, where they were going through the *Love & Respect* book. The pastor gave a message about one of the topics discussed in the book. Afterwards, we had time to share with other couples at our table. A wife at our table asked the group how to respect her husband. My husband responded to her that respect is about respecting the position, such as respecting our president because he holds that position. My husband also referenced his time in the Navy and how he respected the position of those who were in charge. This was a new perspective for me because I didn't think I had been respecting the position that my husband has in our home.

God gave my husband authority over our family. That means I have to swallow my pride and submit to my husband's God-given authority in our home. If I'm honest, I think that I always know what is best for our family. This is the sin of pride in my life. God is asking me to respect my husband's authority and his position as head of our household. Now if God is asking me to do this, I am more willing to comply than if my husband asked me to do this. I do not like being told what to do (again, my pride). God is chipping away at this stubborn pride of mine and showing me a better way.

Respecting my husband is honoring the Lord. It is how I can obey the Lord in my life, not obeying my husband per se, but obeying the Lord. When I am honoring God by respecting my husband, my husband can then, in turn, love me.

The dynamic of marriage was orchestrated by God. He knew that we would have to depend on Him to honor our spouses. We cannot do it on our own. I've been striving to be the perfect wife, but when I look at marriage through the eyes of God, He has asked me to respect my husband. Not be perfect, but be respectful. I need to do the thing that God has asked me to do, not my idea of what would work best or what I think being a perfect wife looks like.

My husband really loves me and shows me in many little ways. The least I can do is respect him in return. The truth is my husband is honoring God by loving me, and I'm the one who needs to honor God by respecting my husband. I need to stop pointing the finger and change my attitude. That way, both of us will honor God in our marriage. And isn't that what I really want, a God-honoring marriage? Yes I do.

Chapter 9
Zip Your Lips

I read verses in the Bible about submitting and respect. I know most of them by heart, but I keep learning by applying them. It seems that putting these truths into practice really works. And as silly as it seems, God cares about the details in our lives. He rewards our obedience to Him. Every single time.

My husband and I take hikes together on Saturday mornings. We started doing this a few months ago, and it has become a great time to communicate. Especially since we are hiking next to each other and not having to keep eye contact the whole time. I think this helps communication because you can talk more honestly while walking next to your spouse. Sometimes our faces betray us while we are listening, and the trust is broken. This way, the communication lines are wide open.

On our hike this past Saturday, I wanted to put into practice this idea about keeping quiet so that your husband can share. I read about this in the book *Love & Respect,* by Dr. Emerson Eggerichs. Now, I talk a lot. My sweet husband is very kind to listen to me. So on this hike, I decided not to initiate any conversation. I was just going to follow my husband as we walked and let him lead the conversation. It seemed easy enough. Once, again, I have so much to learn.

Right away, I wanted to say something. But I stuck to my guns and kept my mouth shut. We walked quietly for a while, and then my husband started talking. At first it was about our surroundings and the things we saw as we walked. He pointed out a trail that was off the beaten path and asked me if we should go on an adventure and follow it. I agreed, and we took our adventure walk. It was a lot more fun walking on a new path. We even saw that someone had bent back the fencing next to a huge sign that declared, "No Trespassing." It was tempting, but my husband continued to lead us on our adventure path. It was so nice to do something new together.

Then as we walked more, he began talking about work and how he was encouraging another coworker who was struggling. Next he shared more about different topics. It was so wonderful to hear about his life. I guess I never gave him a chance to share. I was stunned because I thought I was good at taking turns in our conversations. But truly, by keeping my mouth shut, I was able to look into my husband's life and see what his daily grind was like. Normally, I'm focused on my own daily life, not even considering his.

What else was great about listening and giving space for my husband to share was that now I can join him in prayer for those needs that he or his coworkers face. I can be a part of the solution and not part of the problem. By listening, I can relate to my husband better and understand where he is coming from. Plus, we were outside, enjoying the sun as we hiked, and getting a little exercise while learning more about each other.

The best part of our hour-long hike was that when I was silent, he would say out loud to me, "I love you." In that hour, he said, "I love you," eleven times. Boy, do I need to keep my mouth shut more often!

Chapter 10
The Art of Submitting

I am not the spiritual leader of our home. I have been fired. The truth is, I felt like I was supposed to do that job. I'm the mom. I take care of our kids and read them devotions in the morning and Bible stories before bed. That's what I do. But that is not what God created me to do. God created me to love Him with all my heart and to respect my husband. Why then do I feel like I just lost my job?

God's Word cuts to the heart of the matter every time. I am in a place where God has shown me the error of my ways, and He is redirecting me. My error was thinking that it was my job to be the spiritual leader. That job was created by God for my husband to do. Just because I didn't think he was doing that job doesn't mean I was supposed to take that job position. Once again, big error on my part. Giant error on my part.

Respecting my husband means I submit to him and his leadership in our home. His leadership role also includes being the spiritual leader. My husband loves me, loves our kids, and takes our family to church every Sunday. He reads his Bible every morning. He tithes. He is doing his job as the spiritual leader of our home. In my sinfulness, I admit that I didn't think he was doing his job, so I assumed the position. Pride is the worst sin of all. Who do I think I am? I obviously thought my job was to do a little more than what my husband was doing. I was wrong once again.

The funny part is that I was the only one who thought it was my job to do all those things. I gave myself the job and the job title, and I thought I was doing a pretty great job as well. Only through putting submission and respect into practice did I realize that I had gotten way off track. God opened my eyes slowly to His truth. His ways are not my ways.

> For my thoughts are not your thoughts, neither are
> your ways my ways, declares the Lord. (Isaiah 55:8)

The truth hurts. I feel like I'm fired from a job that I gave to myself. The facts are that job was never mine, and my husband was already doing it. I just created this idea in my head that I should do that job. It was not true. It did not help my children. It did not help me. And it definitely did not help my husband.

God kindly showed me that I am a sinner, saved by His grace. I can embrace my true job description, which is to love the Lord with all my heart and soul and mind and strength. And to love my neighbor as myself. That is what God has called me to do. Oh, and submit to my husband too.

Chapter 11
Submission Protects You

I love how God teaches us through so many ways. I've been soaking in the fact the more I submit to my husband, the more he steps up and takes care of basically everything. I feel awkward as to what my role is as a wife. But the beauty of submission is that it's truly for my own protection. Submission is for my safety. God revealed the truth of this through a book titled *Outlander* by Diana Gabaldon. Think of Scotland, hillsides of lavender, and burly men.

In the middle of the book, a young married couple are learning about each other. The wife is from the future, and her current husband has no clue. She married him because she is English and he is Scottish, and his clan thinks she's a spy. She married him for protection.

Needless to say, a woman from the 1900s has a different viewpoint of marriage than a woman from the 1700s. So her new husband expects her to obey him. As they are escaping from the English on horseback, the husband tells his wife to stay in a safe area with her horse, while he goes with men from his clan to meet up with some allies. He tells her that he cannot fight the enemy and keep her safe at the same time. He also tells her that if she leaves before he returns, he will punish her.

Well, we all know what she did. The minute she was left alone, she took off to find her own way back. She really believed that she knew best. As she walked into the Highlands, the English captured her and took her to their commander. As she was about to be throttled by the English commander, her husband appeared to rescue her. And yes, they survived and escaped; it is a love story after all. What took place once they were safe was what was so remarkable to me.

When they are safely at an inn for the night, the husband said that because she took off from the safe area, she not only put herself and him in danger, she put all his men in danger too. Her one choice to do what she thought was best put their whole group in danger. What she did was selfish and willful, and she did not think of the consequences. Especially since he was trying to protect her in the first place. The husband said he had to punish her because it was just. He was following through on what he told her. He told her that all his men needed justice served because of how her actions put them at risk. Her one act affected so many people. It was a life-or-death situation.

What I took away from this exchange was that the things my husband says and does are to protect me. I spend much of my time doing what I think is best, and I probably would have taken off from the safe area like the woman in the story did. Yet our husbands are making decisions in our lives to protect us. God made them protectors and defenders. There is a reason that they behave the way they do. It is to my detriment that I rebel against my husband's directives. My husband is basing his decisions on what is best to protect me and our family.

When did I get so bent on the idea that I am my own protector? Do I think I am stronger than my husband? My actions seem to indicate that I believe this way. The truth is I am weak. I could not physically fight someone and win. I could not physically protect my kids alone. I can't even scream really loudly. I don't look intimidating at all. Yet I behave like I am the protector when clearly I am not.

This wrong thinking needs to change. God has a reason that husbands protect and wives nurture. It is the way God designed us. Living the way God designed us is how we feel the most satisfied and truly at peace. Living in rebellion to God's truth only leads to disappointment and failure. I don't want to fail. God's Word says that when I abide in Him, I cannot keep on sinning.

God protects us in every way, but He is a gentleman and gave us our own wills. We choose to serve Him. Part of that choice means that as I abide in the Lord, I am doing what His Word says to do. His Word says to respect my husband, and it's for my own good. For my own protection. I'm going to abide in the Lord and respect my husband. Only good can come out of that. I want good in my life. I want the peace that passes understanding. It's the best way to live.

Chapter 12
God's Favor

For you bless the righteous, O Lord; you cover him with favor as with a shield.

—Psalm 5:12

God's favor. It's what we want, isn't it? When we were on our family trip to Hawaii, it was this verse that blessed me the whole time. God's favor on our lives is like a shield. His goodness is there to protect us. Part of the blessing of submitting to the Lord is the benefit of His favor, His shield on our lives. God blesses us constantly, and when we stand still to receive it, we are filled with His peace.

During our amazing trip to Oahu, I chose to relax. I say this because normally, I'm so preoccupied with taking care of everything and everyone. Since God has been working on my heart to submit to my husband, I let him take care of all the details of our trip. My husband went above and beyond. The entire trip we had God's favor upon us. I was still in "relaxed mode" when we returned home. I realize that this choice to trust God and surrender to Him is for my benefit.

Choosing to trust God, submit and respect my husband keeps benefiting me. It seems unreal to me that I see such quick results when I surrender to the Lord. I think it's because I am changing from the inside out and putting God's Word into practice. It's not just lip service. It's living out the Word of God.

Halfway through our family vacation, the toilet lid broke in the bathroom. Normally, I would have been totally stressing out about telling the owners of the Airbnb, wondering what they were going to do and how much we'd have to pay, and so on. But instead, I told my husband that the lid broke, and he said he'd take care of it. He said that he saw an extra toilet seat in the closet, and he would replace it. In the past, I would have listened to him but still stressed out until everything was taken care of. I made a different decision this time. I trusted that my husband would take care of it, and I let it go. I let it go even mentally. I continued to enjoy our beautiful vacation in Hawaii. Let me tell you, it felt so good to let go.

The best part of putting God's Word of trust and submission into practice is that not only am I blessed with peace, my husband is blessed also. Before we left the Airbnb, my husband replaced the toilet seat and texted the owners about it. When the owners responded, they thanked my husband for taking care of it and refunded him fifty dollars! My husband was rewarded for doing the right thing. He took care of it. Just like he told me he would. My husband is amazing!

What I am learning is that God's favor is on us all the time. We can choose to be patient and appreciate it, or wait for the other shoe to drop. It's our perceptions of things that make the difference. We need to trust and obey God's Word. He is going to take care of everything in His time. That's where patience comes in. We need to wait on the Lord and be thankful for His shield of protection. He takes care of every need and then some.

Conclusion

Submit to God, and He will take care of the rest. Once we understand that God is God and we are not, we can walk the narrow path in front of us. Don't stray to the wide path that leads to destruction. Keep your eyes on Jesus, submit to your husband, and love each other. If we really focus on doing things God's way, His peace will fill our hearts. His yoke is easy and light. Walk in love and embrace the peace of God that passes understanding.

This truth about submission was illustrated to me when my family and I rode a double surrey bike rental around Doheny State Beach. A double surrey has four seats. Each passenger can pedal, but only the driver's wheel actually steers. My husband sat in the driver's seat, and I sat next to him. The wheel in front of me was spinning endlessly, while my husband's wheel steered the double surrey around the sidewalk along the beach. No matter how I spun my wheel, we still went the way my husband steered. And believe me, I was steering my wheel to turn when I wanted to turn, yet we stayed the course that my husband set. My husband was leading our family as we pedaled together. Just the way God intended.

This was the final lesson in submission. No matter what you

do or how many times you spin your wheel, God is in control. Let that beautiful truth sink into your mind. Take a deep breath, and trust in the Lord. Submit because that is the way that God wants you to go. And remember—*submit* is not a four-letter word anymore.

Additional Tips

Tip 1: Trust God with your marriage (Ephesians 5:22). Pay attention to how you respond to your husband.

Tip 2: Pray for wisdom (Proverbs 2:6). Get on your knees, and pray about the specific areas that you need God to give you wisdom about.

Tip 3: Put submission into practice (Ephesians 5:33; 1 Peter 3:1–2). Walk by faith and not by sight. Don't look at the donkeys; look to Jesus (1 Samuel 9:20).

Printed in the United States
By Bookmasters